# The COLLEGE Admissions Handbook

## SOPHIE GIBBONS

*The College Admissions Handbook*

First Edition

Copyright © 2025 by Apricity Publishing.

ISBN: 979-8-9899069-7-0

Library of Congress Control Number: 2024922415

Published by Apricity Publishing
Wiscasset, Maine
ApricityPublishing.com


Printed in the United States

# Acknowledgements

Just as it takes a posse to complete your college applications, it takes a village to write a book like this. We want to begin by acknowledging the work of Kathryn Storke, who wrote the original edition of *The College Admissions Workbook* in 2003.

We would like to thank Megan Donnelly, who taught at Northfield Mt. Hermon in the English department and has written many a recommendation letter. Her expertise around college interviews was invaluable.

We would like to thank everyone we sourced without whom this book would not have been as fruitful.

Sophie would like to thank Gigi Frye for her guidance through her college application journey.

Additionally, we would like to thank the Apricity Publishing team, Frances Pearson for her leadership around our Blue 2 Media team, Kelly for her design work, and Jonathan for his editing skills.

# Dedication

We dedicate this book to those who are striving to get the best education they can by dedicating their time to find the right college for them – and then committing to the process, however challenging, to say they left no stone unturned in their quest for the right college fit for them.

# Table of Contents

# Introduction
## The Why

Does the world really need another college admissions book, we asked ourselves? Why yes, it does, because the admissions process, to say nothing of the nuances around getting your application seen, taken seriously, and truly considered is not a level playing field. There are legacies; those who have parents, grandparents, sisters, cousins, and who knows who else, that have the inside track on how to get in. Money? If you have money for private tutors (yes, SAT and ACT tutors abound), you will score better. Score better, and you will make the cutoff to be considered. Recommendations? If you spent the first sixteen years of your life cast away on a deserted island and no one knows your name, let alone can write a recommendation, the admissions person might just think it was your lackluster personality that gave you no one to vouch for you. The bottom line? Our intention in writing this is to give you the support—in all areas of the application process—that you need to compete. Like it or not, it's a competition, and you need a team behind you. That's us. Your Team Me coaches, cheerleaders, and wise personage who have been here before you, traveling the road you must travel to get to the finish line.

Buckle up. Worry not. We have your back. It's all here. And, if you know someone who needs this book and can't afford it, just send us an email at Inquiry@ApricityPublishing.com with their name and address, and it will be in the mail before you can yell, "I got into my first choice!"

# Your College Admissions Posse

## Sophie Gibbons, The Applicant

My dream school was… I didn't have one. There was not one school that I was dying to attend. My college application process began my junior year of high school, but the preparation really started in 9th grade. From the ripe old age of 14, I was asked what I wanted to do with my life and more specifically where I wanted to go to college. Let's keep in mind that I still wore jean shorts over my leggings at this point. Given my high school class was over 700 students and there were only about four or five college counselors for all of them, I began working with a private college counselor. To begin, I took a survey that helped her get to know me better and get to know what I was looking for in a college. I knew I wanted a big university, preferably outside of California, where I grew up, and one with strong academics, athletics, and a prominent social life. These specifications guided my search and together my advisor and I narrowed my college list down to 13-15 schools. I sent applications out to all 15 and eagerly awaited their response. My application year was unique because it was during the height of the COVID-19 pandemic. I was unable to visit any of the colleges in person. While I probably would have had a top choice had I been able to visit in-person, at the time I didn't really care. My mentality was to pick my favorite college based on the ones I was accepted to. And for me, this process worked. I am a rising junior at the University of Michigan and I believe this is truly where I was meant to go.

My story is just one example of how the college process is unique. You get to decide what you like, what you don't like, and where you want to go. Reflecting on my college application experience, I see how having a private college advisor changed the game for me. Had I not had the help I did I would have been completely lost. I realize not many people have the opportunity to access a hands-on college advisor at a large public high school and even fewer have the luxury to hire a private college advisor. This is why a book like this is so important and impactful.

Whether you choose to go through the college process like I did or not, it is helpful to be armed with the knowledge to make the best decision for yourself. Inside of this handbook, you will find the essential information you will need to successfully go through the college process.

## Christine Merser, The Parent

The first inkling I had as to what we were dealing with came in the spring of our daughter's freshman year in high school, when she came home chastising her father and me for not signing her up for the Biology SAT II test. "All the other parents care about where their kids are going to go to college, and you don't!"

I immediately got on the phone and found out that not only was she right—all the other kids were taking the SAT II exams— but they were also already working with SAT tutors, as well as outside advisors counseling their families on their ideal course loads. Now, we need to acknowledge that our daughter was attending a competitive private school in New York City, where parents were always pushing their children to pursue what they thought were the best educational and extracurricular activities available. As a person who went to a public high school in Michigan, and whose parents had no idea where I even applied to college, I really was not prepared for all this.

So began our participation in the Kentucky Derby of college races—with the finish line set for April 1. (The cruelty of the date was not lost on me, and I assure you there was not one April Fools' joke made in our home regarding college acceptances.)

The final day of reckoning was drama-filled, with emotions running higher than I thought possible; there was crying, screaming, phoning, emailing, and texting as our daughter, along with all her peers, logged into the admissions pages of their coveted schools the minute the results became available. Some decision letters were mailed, too. Our daughter (and this touches my soul) took the acceptances that came early in the week, before the letter from her first choice arrived, and put them on a chair in the hallway of our apartment building, sure that the positive Feng Shui would bring her the envelope she wanted.

I've had a lot of time since that day years ago to think about college acceptances and what they actually mean. A friend once told me that if he'd gone to Princeton or Yale, his life would have been different. The connections he would have gained by attending those fine institutions would have opened up a different kind of success—the kind you can only get by knowing the right people—which could have changed what was possible for his future. And he's right; it's true that that does happen.

Then there's the odd duck who says that they specifically chose a lesser-known institution because it attracted well-rounded people, and that they've had a happier life for doing so. That can also be true.

Then there are all the editorials saying that no one asks where you went to college after college is over, and that the name of the institution on your diploma doesn't matter. Not so true, in my opinion, but I get what they mean.

Truth be told, where you should go to college depends on who you are and what you want in life. But no matter who you are, it does matter. Perhaps not primarily for any of the reasons listed above, but rather because it is the first major evaluation that reflects on who you are and how the wider world will see you. It is the first real time the outside world holds you up to a measuring stick and informs you of your worth. The results of the college application process will be broadcast to your friends, teachers, and family—and can affect how you see yourself for a long time afterward.

I saw this with my child, whose worth was already so very great before her college acceptances, but who received congratulations from those in our community with a renewed sense of awe and respect. They already thought she was smart—but now they knew it. After all, it had been verified by the admissions department, those faceless yet oh-so-powerful individuals who spent all of one hour with her and read her application amid a raging sea of others.

So, what's the lesson I've learned? How would I do it differently?

There is only one thing I would do. I would spend a lot more time before and during this process talking to her about the markers that the outside world judges us by—and how this is one of the major flaws of our society. I would sing of her sense of inner worth and help her understand how it can only be nurtured from within, not from acceptance letters on the stoop. "Easy for her to say," I can hear you thinking. "Her daughter made the cut."

That's true, and when she got those acceptance letters, I was more relieved than you know. But it wasn't because I thought the schools were that much greater; it was because I knew it meant so much to her self-image, and I was thrilled that others saw her the same way she saw herself.

6

But the big lesson has to do with how to approach it all. There are so many tricks of the trade, and what I have come to realize is that without the right resources and guidance to help you through the process, it's easy to get lost, or miss opportunities. You need information—lots of it—from a trusted source who can show you which stones to turn over, when to do what, and how to approach the dizzying array of options.

Well, I happen to own a publishing company. We publish select books that we believe have worth, and we market them. And so here we are, launching *The College Admissions Handbook*, an easy-to-read, concrete, comprehensive handbook designed to guide you through every step of the college application process. We present this book with pride, and in the certainty that it will help students and parents navigate the complicated, over-crowded waters of college admissions.

One of my daughter's friends had already suffered the loss of her mother, among other challenges, when she was applying to colleges. At a gathering of friends celebrating and lamenting the results of their decision letters, I heard her say, "I'm just happy I'm going to college." May you all remember her words throughout this process, and be mindful of the fact that the value of the student does not depend on the validation of some unknown admissions advisor who can't possibly appreciate the true worth of the person whose application they hold in the palms of their hands. Good luck. For those getting ready to apply to colleges, we know you can present your best self and attend the college that will jump-start the next chapter of your life.

# Chapter 1.
# Your Posse: The Cast of Characters

*" The nicest thing about teamwork is that
you always have others on your side."*

–Margaret Carty

Applying to college, and gaining admission, is not a one-person show. It involves a cast of people, who will (hopefully) do their part to increase your chances of admission to the college of your choice.

# Lead Roles

## You!

You play the lead in this film. You are also the director, the writer, the creative director, and, and, and. It's exhausting being you. It's important to realize that this is perhaps the first time you can't start this whole assignment the night before it's due. Nope. Not this time. The longer you have to prepare, the better you will appear to those faceless decision-makers. So, set that procrastinator inside aside. She isn't invited to this filmmaking project.

But, while you do have the biggest role, you are not alone. You must build your posse, those around you that are on team **YOU**.

Let's review the cast of characters.

## Your College Counselor

Your new best friend. Your co-star. They have the power to make or break your application. Their recommendation counts ... a lot. If you are reading this when you are a sophomore, start building a relationship with your college counselor now. If you are further along, get on it first thing. Most high schools assign you a college counselor but if your school allows you to pick one, ask your friends, ask a favorite teacher which one they think would be a good fit.

Then GOOGLE them and see what they care about. Make sure they know who you are. Introduce yourself, with humor and sincerity. Be you. Ask a friend who has that advisor to introduce you. If your school allows you to ask for a specific advisor, do your homework to know which one you want to call yours.

Be careful though. Don't be too pushy. Too intrusive. Too all about you. You don't want a court injunction that says you have to stay 10 feet away from the poor soul.

## Your Parents

This process is not painless, but it doesn't have to be as stressful as it often is. So, mostly, your parents' role will be to help you keep an open mind, and to help you keep from losing your mind. They can also help you to stay organized and stick to deadlines.

# Supporting Cast

- **Your Teachers**

   You will want these to be teachers who know you well, and who are good writers. They will be the ones to write your most influential recommendations. They know you from class, and what kind of student you are is reflected in the letters they write.

- **Your English Teacher**

   Your English teacher will proofread your application and your essay. If you have paid attention in their class, they won't have any corrections.

- **Tutors**

   If you have the resources, tutors can play a vital role in helping you stay organized and achieve high grades and high test scores. If a private tutor isn't in your budget, look into peer tutoring at your high school.

- **Rich Uncle**

   Just kidding!

- **Friends**

  Friends are also members of your posse. You are probably all going through the application process at the same time. This can be a real bonding experience for you all. While we know it's so hard not to compare yourself and think "oh but so and so got in there," don't compare scores, wins, or losses but rather talk about how you are feeling about the process or how an acceptance or rejection made you feel.

**Everyone will start thinking about college applications at different times, but it is important that you start forming your posse as early as possible. The longer they know you as the extraordinary human you are the better.**

# Workbook Time!

Let's set some goals now. What are five things you want to keep in mind as you go through the application process?

1) _____

_____

_____

2) _____

_____

_____

3) _____

_____

_____

4) _____

_____

_____

5) _____

_____

_____

# Chapter 2.
# In the Beginning: Getting Ready to Apply

*" If you give me eight hours to cut down a tree,*
*I will spend the first six sharpening the axe."*

–Abraham Lincoln

Getting ready to push send has a host of moving parts, from essay writing to the common application, to transcript uploads, to recommendation letters, to search and choose which colleges to apply to, and the list goes on. Get a notebook. Keep notes, and revise to do lists. Get a calendar and mark the deadline dates (and give yourself reminders leading up to those deadline dates.) Most of the work you need to do, no one will see.

## PREPARATION: CREATING A TO DO LIST LONGER THAN YOUR LIFE SPAN

❑ Your high school curriculum (Chapter 2)

❑ Your high school activities (Chapter 2)

❑ Testing (Chapter 3)

❑ Choosing your applicant pool (Chapter 4)

❑ Recommendation letters (Chapter 7)

❑ The application (Chapter 5)

# Your High School Curriculum

It is important to remember that your biggest job in preparing to apply for college is to get the best grades you can in the toughest classes you can handle. It isn't easy. In fact, it's hard work. If you have the option of taking regular Statistics or AP Statistics, pick the AP as long as it doesn't cause you to panic. Push yourself, but never close to the edge. Just started reading this book and that curriculum ship has sailed? Don't worry about it. Did you focus on social issues the first two years of high school at the expense of your grades? Don't worry about it. Begin now. Focus on the now. If you show what you are capable of and show the progress that makes you a candidate for your first choice, you have a shot. It's never too late. You can do well. Colleges want to see that you challenge yourself, but they also want to see good grades.

Enthusiasm is important — enjoy school!

# Your High School Activities

In ninth grade, or sooner, find one or more activities outside of the classroom that you enjoy, and which you are willing to devote a significant amount of time to. And stick with it. Colleges want to see consistency. Spending five hours a week on one activity is better than one hour a week on five activities. Colleges want to see commitment. By the time you are applying to colleges, you should have two or three activities to which you have been consistently committed.

Volunteer at a shelter. Walk dogs at your local animal shelter. Volunteer for a political campaign. Tutor younger students in a part of town that needs you.

Love to write? Write stories and send them in. Love to do math? Ask to sit in a college course at a local college. Love science? Go see Oppenheimer and write a film review for the school newspaper. Or offer to do graphic work on the school newspaper, or take photos for the paper. Do what you love and make it work for you.

**TOO MANY EXTRACURRICULAR ACTIVITIES?**

# The Common Application

You've probably heard little whisperings about the Common Application but what is it really? The Common Application is one application that most colleges use. This means instead of writing out all of your extracurriculars, clubs and activities for every individual school, you can input all of that information on one application and send it out to all of the colleges you are applying to, unless they don't accept the Common Application.

## 5 THINGS TO REMEMBER WHEN COMPLETING THE COMMON APPLICATION

1. Make sure to proofread carefully.

2. Remember to complete the future plans section.

3. Always make sure to do the optional essay. Even though it says optional, it really isn't.

4. Remember to save your work before closing the tab. This is a common mistake that people make and they often lose a lot of their work.

5. Remember to submit on time. You put so much work into the Common Application, don't forget to submit it on time.

*Content from Ingenius Prep*

You must submit the Common Application to all schools that require it. Some don't, but most do require it. Additionally, colleges require supplemental, which are more specific essays to the school. Look at each specific college application for these prompts.

### Application Fee Assistance

Most schools charge an application fee and applying to eight+ schools can get expensive. Here are six ways to receive a fee waiver for college applications

## Application Fee Assistance

Most schools charge an application fee and applying to eight+ schools can get expensive. Here are six ways to receive a fee waiver for college applications

### 6 WAYS TO GET A FEE WAIVER

1) Get an SAT or ACT waiver

2) Apply for Common App fee waiver

3) Apply for NACAC Application fee waiver

4) Apply for Coalition App Fee Waiver

5) Ask the College for a Fee Waiver

6) Apply to Colleges without Application Fees

*Content from Best Colleges.*
*All of the links for these waivers are available through*
*www.bestcolleges.com/resources/how-to-get-college-application-fee-waiver/*

Something else that will help you with almost every part of your application process is reading. Read books on topics that matter to you. Not at the third grade level. Stretch yourself. Ask the librarian at school what book to take out based on what you say are your interests. This will improve your vocabulary and reading comprehension, two major components of the SAT and ACT. Reading *The New York Times*, or *Forbes Magazine*, or *Ms Magazine*, or your local paper weekly, will also improve your reading comprehension, as well as give you things to write about in your essay. It will also show interviewers that you know what's going on in the world. Colleges like students who are aware.

If you are so inclined, you might want to keep a journal. It will improve your writing skills while also keeping a record of what is going on in your life. By the time you begin writing your college application essay, your journal will be full of ideas.

# Reading List

Some intelligent books (as in, not romance or true crime novels) are:

- *A Confederacy of Dunces* by John Kennedy Toole

- *Catch 22* by Joseph Heller

- *The Lexus and the Olive Tree* by Thomas L. Friedman

- *One Hundred Years of Solitude* by Gabriel García Márquez

- *Song of Solomon* by Toni Morrison

- *To Kill a Mockingbird* by Harper Lee

- For parents: Bob Clagett, Senior Admissions Officer at Harvard recommends **The College Admissions Mystique** by Bill Mayher. He calls it "anxiety diffusing."

# Helpful Websites

- You can subscribe online to *The New York Times*, free of charge, at www.nytimes.com

- Find out which APs are offered at www.collegeboard.com/ap/students/subjects.html

- https://ingeniusprep.com/blog/common-app-mistakes/

- https://www.bestcolleges.com/resources/how-to-get-college-application-fee-waiver/

# Workbook Time!

Write down some of your hobbies.

_____

_____

_____

_____

_____

Which of these hobbies can you take leadership roles in?

_____

_____

_____

_____

Write down some AP classes that you can take in the coming years.

_____

_____

_____

_____

_____

# Chapter 3.
# Testing...1, 2, 3: The SAT, ACT, and Test-Optional Policies

*" If you think you can do a thing or think you can't do a thing, you're right."*

— Henry Ford

Colleges still use numbers to help them make decisions, but standardized testing is no longer a one-size-fits-all metric. While many colleges have gone test-optional, your SAT or ACT scores can still be important for certain schools or scholarships. The landscape of standardized testing has changed significantly, and it's important to know what to expect.

# SAT versus ACT

| | SAT | ACT |
|---|---|---|
| **Why Take It** | Used for college admissions and merit-based scholarships | Used for college admissions and merit-based scholarships |
| **Test Structure** | Reading, Writing & Language, Math | English, Math, Reading, Science Reasoning |
| **Essay** | No essay option (discontinued 2021) | No essay option (discontinued) |
| **Test Length** | 3 hours | 2 hours, 55 minutes (without essay) |
| **Number of Questions** | 154 questions | 215 questions |
| **Reading Section** | 5 reading passages | 4 reading passages |
| **Science Section** | None | 1 science section testing critical thinking (not specific science knowledge) |
| **Math Content** | Arithmetic, Algebra I & II, Geometry, Trigonometry, Data Analysis | Arithmetic, Algebra I & II, Geometry, Trigonometry, Probability, Statistics |
| **Calculator Policy** | Calculator only allowed on certain math questions | Calculator allowed on all math questions |
| **How It's Scored** | Scored on a scale of 400-1600 | Scored on a scale of 1-36 |
| **Superscoring** | Available at many schools (check specific college policies) | Available at many schools (check specific college policies) |
| **Cost** | $60 (fee waivers available) | $66 (fee waivers available) |

*Source: Princeton Review (https://www.princetonreview.com/college/sat-act)*

# Test-Optional Trend

In recent years, many colleges have moved to **test-optional policies**, which means you are not required to submit SAT or ACT scores with your application. This shift started before, but expanded after COVID-19. While some schools are still fully test-optional, others might recommend or require test scores for specific programs or scholarships.

# What Should You Do?

- **Check Requirements:** Go to the admissions pages of the schools you're applying to and confirm whether they require test scores.

- **Submit Great Scores:** If you excelled on the SAT or ACT, submit your scores, as it may strengthen your application.

- **Skip if Average:** If you feel your test scores don't represent your academic abilities, don't worry! You can focus on other aspects of your application, like essays and extracurriculars.

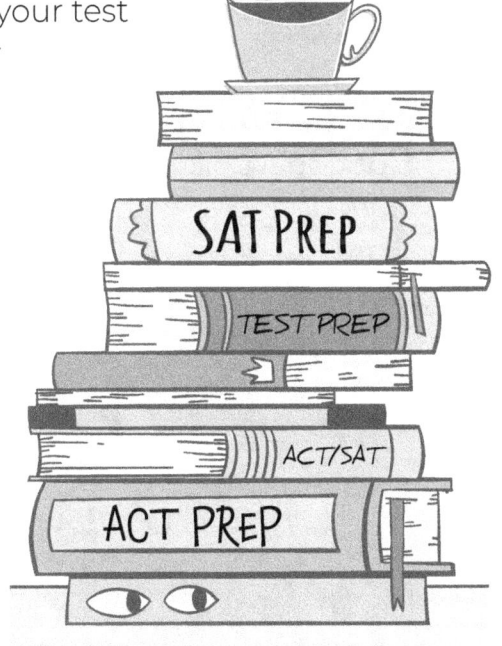

- **Superscoring:** Many schools allow you to "superscore," which means they will take your best section scores across multiple test attempts to create a higher composite score.

# The Good News

- **Test-Optional Policies are Widespread:** Many schools now allow students to apply without test scores, especially in the wake of the pandemic. This means that if standardized testing isn't your strong suit, you can still present a competitive application.

- **Superscoring Can Boost Results:** For both the SAT and ACT, superscoring lets you combine your best section scores from multiple test attempts, which can lead to a higher overall score. This is a big advantage if you've taken the test more than once.

- **Practice Improves Scores:** While you can't "study" for the SAT or ACT in the traditional sense, regular practice does help. Platforms like Khan Academy offer free SAT prep, and ACT also offers plenty of free resources to improve your chances.

- **Fewer Students are Taking the SAT/ACT:** With test-optional policies becoming more common, fewer students are opting to take these tests. If you choose to submit a great score, it could set you apart from others.

If you have a great score, submit it, because it could strengthen your application. To see which schools are test optional, go to fairtest.org/test-optional-list/

# The Bad News

- **A High Score Isn't a Guarantee:** Even students with top SAT or ACT scores aren't guaranteed admission to selective schools. Colleges look at your entire application, including essays, extracurriculars, and recommendations.

- **Test Scores Still Matter for Some Schools:** While test-optional policies are widespread, many competitive colleges still give weight to your SAT or ACT scores, especially for merit-based scholarships or honors programs.

- **The Playing Field is Uneven:** Standardized tests still tend to favor students from better-resourced schools or those who can afford expensive test prep services. This systemic bias is why many students opt not to submit scores when they aren't required.

- **Test-Optional Doesn't Mean Test-Blind:** Even if a college is test-optional, submitting strong scores can still work in your favor. If you don't submit scores, it might leave admissions officers questioning how you would have performed.

# Preparing for the SAT or ACT

- **Practice, Don't Cram:** While you can't "study" for the SAT or ACT in the traditional sense, you can practice, practice, practice! Use resources like **10 Real SATs** by College Board or **Getting Into the ACT** by ACT.

- **Take the PSAT:** If you're leaning toward the SAT, take the PSAT first. It's a great way to familiarize yourself with the SAT format and even qualify for the National Merit Scholarship.

- **Use Online Resources:** Many test-prep platforms offer free practice tests, like those at Princeton Review or Khan Academy, which partners with College Board for SAT practice.

## WHAT TO BRING TO THE TEST

- ❏ A photo ID. A drivers' license or school ID is best, but if you realize the night before the test that you don't have a photo ID, a passport will also do the trick.

- ❏ Three Number 2 pencils, a good eraser, and a calculator.

- ❏ Your admission ticket. The College Board sends this to you after you have registered for the test.

- ❏ Remember to have a good breakfast, since food and drink aren't allowed at the test.

Remember to keep some perspective about these tests. They are not the end of the world, so you shouldn't put the energy into them as if they were. Focus your efforts on your classes, especially since that is the best way for you to prepare for the other tests you will have to take. Yes, that's right. More tests.

Most colleges also require or recommend three SAT II subject tests: one in math, the Writing test, and an additional test of your choice. As a ninth grader, you should find out which SAT II tests are offered, so that you can plan on taking them right after you have finished the course, when the information is fresh in your mind. Go to www.collegeboard.com/student/testing/sat/about/SATII.html to find out which tests are offered. You should only take the tests you are prepared for. Do not take tests just to take them, as colleges will see all of your SAT II scores. Check out your local bookstore or online to find test prep books for each subject.

You are not, however, required to send all your Advanced Placement, or AP, scores. You can choose to send only those that you do well on. The best way to do well on the APs is to study hard for your class. There are students at one of the toughest high schools in California who worked very hard to receive B's in their AP Spanish Language class, and who ended up scoring 5's on the AP. Your hard work will pay off.

## Reading List

- **10 Real SATs** by College Board. A must-have for SAT preparation.

- **Getting Into the ACT** by ACT: Similar to *10 Real SATs*, but for the ACT.

- Any SAT/ACT prep book by Barron's, Kaplan, or Princeton Review.

# Helpful Websites

- **College Board:** Register for the SAT and find test-prep resources: www.collegeboard.com

- **ACT:** Register for the ACT and take practice tests: www.act.org

- **FairTest:** To see a list of test-optional schools: www.fairtest.org

- **Khan Academy:** Free SAT practice tests and prep: www.khanacademy.org

# Chapter 4.
# Pick a College, Any College: Where Do You Belong?

*" You have brains in your head. You have feet in your shoes. You can steer yourself, in any direction you choose."*

—Dr. Seuss

## Getting Your Mindset Together

Sometimes in the college admissions process you will feel like your life is at the mercy of the admissions committees. Or your parents' vision for you. Or, your college advisor's misinterpretation of your potential. And while it is true that they are choosing who they want at their school, you have just as much power in deciding which schools you want to grace with your application. And, you can learn a great life lesson in compromise and picking your battles. You can apply to the college your parents went to, even if you have no desire to go there, and you can wait until all the acceptances are in, and deal with it at that time. You can ask your advisor to include the colleges you want along with the safety schools they think are 'right' for you.

Remember, you are the director, you have more control than you think you do. But picking your battles is best done after the process is complete.

# Searching for the Perfect Fit

Before beginning the search process, figure out what you like and don't like in a college. Do you want a big school or small school? Do you want a college town or city? What are you interested in studying? What extracurricular activities do you want to participate in? Thinking about all of these questions will help you narrow down your search and make the following steps a lot easier.

## PICK A SCHOOL, ANY SCHOOL!

### I DON'T KNOW WHICH TO PICK!

So how do you go about deciding which colleges you should apply to? Finding the colleges that meet your list of criteria is the ticket.

That means research.

Getting to know the colleges will help you in more ways than one: it will let you know if it's where you want to be, and it will help you appear knowledgeable when answering such application or interview questions as "Why do you want to attend University X?" Colleges want students who want them, and they want to know why you want them. In fact, this is why legacy applicants have an advantage: because they are more likely to know the school, and more likely to really want to attend.

Getting started you will want a big reference book. We recommend **The Fiske Guide to Colleges** by Edward Fiske. It is updated every year, and it has both general statistics (such as the number of students enrolled and average SAT scores), very honest commentary from students, and other ratings of nearly 300 colleges. Parents: you can think of it as a sort of Zagat Guide to colleges. Use this to get an idea of what's out there. You'll be amazed to learn there's more than just the Ivy League and Local State University.

## HOW TO USE AI TO CREATE A COLLEGE LIST

In your AI browser, start your message by typing in "Here is the criteria I am looking for in a college." Then proceed by adding in all of the criteria you are looking for in a college. Include size, general location (if you know where you want to be), social life qualities, academics, and more. The more specific you are, the better and more accurate the response. In addition to your criteria, add in facts about yourself. Include your high school GPA, ACT/SAT scores, campus involvement, AP and honors classes you've taken, areas of interest, and more. Conclude by saying "Give me 15 colleges that would find me a viable candidate."

# Content from Forbes

Additionally, check out the colleges' own websites. Of course, they are highly promotional, and they show the school in the best possible light, but they have plenty of information. Some even have virtual tours. Also, write to colleges asking to be sent informational literature. Colleges like to see you initiate contact. This request letter might be the first piece to go in your file.

Once you have some sort of idea of what kind of schools interest you, you are going to want to visit colleges, preferably before you apply, but certainly before you accept an offer of admission. By visit, we don't mean walk through campus. Visiting entails quite a bit more effort than that.

# Visit Checklist

### Bare Minimum

If you're pressed for time and you're trying to cram 10 visits into three days (which is why it's wise to start early), the very least you will want to do is take a tour and attend an informational session. It might be tempting to do the minimum, but don't.

# HOW TO ENSURE AN IDEAL VISIT

- Give yourself plenty of time.
- Make an appointment two or three months in advance for an on-campus interview.
- Ask your counselor if anyone from your high school attends.
- Bring your school's ID number (if you don't know it, ask your college counselor).
- Wear comfortable shoes!
- Visit during the school year in the middle of the week. "Visiting in the summer puts undue emphasis on the way the school looks," says Bruce Breimer, college counselor at Collegiate School in New York City.
- Take a tour and pay attention.
- Wander around by yourself. "Look under stones," says Jon Reider, counselor at San Francisco University High School. "Check out parts of the school they don't show you."
- Attend an information session.
- Attend a class but remember that one class isn't necessarily representative of all classes.
- Eat in the dining hall.
- Check out the athletic facilities.
- Read the college newspaper – what's really happening here?
- Scope out bulletin boards on campus.
- Wander around the library.
- Pick up a course catalog.
- Interview with an admissions officer.
- Meet with a professor in your area of interest, if possible.
- Spend the night with a friend or other student.
- Ask questions — try to find sophomores who are close enough to high school, but not brand new to the college.
- Take notes. Make sure your notes will make sense to you a month or more later. What do you like? What don't you like? Why? Can you see yourself in this environment?

# Words of Wisdom

"There might be validity to stereotypes, but it's important to see beyond them. What don't the stereotypes tell you?" says Bob Clagett, Senior Admissions Officer at Harvard University.

Once you've done the research, you can put together your list. Which schools are you going to apply to? You should apply to at least eight schools: two or three "safety" schools, two or three "target" schools, and two or three "reach" schools. How do you know which is which for you? First hint: Harvard is not a safety for anyone. Second hint: your transcript (your grades in high school) is the most important factor in deciding whether or not you will be admitted (which is why your biggest job in high school is to get good grades). Knowing this, you can compare yourself to the freshman class at the colleges. How do your grades and test scores compare? Third hint: a meeting with your college counselor is the best way to figure out which schools fall into which category for you.

In putting together your list, you should know why each college has made the cut. There shouldn't be any schools on your list that you don't want to go to. No school should be on your list just because you know you can get in. It's okay for you to have preferences, but if you can't find more than two schools you want to go to, you haven't done enough research. Get excited about every school on your list!

If you can't visit a school in person, look at their website. Since COVID-19, most schools offer virtual tours. While you can get a better sense of a school in person, a virtual tour is better than nothing. Additionally, look at their social media. Instagram and Facebook can tell you a lot about the student body and other details that aren't mentioned on their website. You can find students' social media as well.

# Reading List

- ***The Fiske Guide to Colleges,*** most recent edition, by Edward B. Fiske. Very helpful, with lots of honest information about many of the nation's best colleges, including quality of life ratings and quotes from current students.

- ***Colleges That Change Lives: 40 Schools You Should Know About Even If You're Not a Straight-A Student*** by Loren Pope. Pope profiles 40 schools you may never have heard of, but whose graduates have a high success rate. Ed Hu, college counselor at Harvard-Westlake, calls them "schools that fly under the radar screen."

- ***Winning the Heart of the College Admissions Dean: An Expert's Advice for Getting into College*** by Joyce Slayton Mitchell. The entire first part of this book is devoted to helping you figure out which colleges are right for you.

# Helpful Websites

- Peterson's is full of college profiles, which you can search by college name, location, size, etc.: www.petersons.com

- Check out Princeton Review's "Counselor-O-Matic" to generate a list of possible colleges: www.princetonreview.com/college/research

- What if you can't visit before you apply? Or what if you need reminding of what it was you saw on your visit? Try www.campustours.com or www.collegiatechoice.com.

- https://www.forbes.com/sites/avivalegatt/2023/04/24/how-to-boost-your-college-applications-using-ai---without-cheating-the-essay/?sh=3002c2d717ef

# Workbook Time!

What are some things that you are looking for in a college?

Think about location, majors offered, size, extracurricular activities, and alumni. What else do you care about?

_____

_____

_____

_____

_____

_____

_____

_____

# Chapter 5
# The Package: Your Application

*" And suddenly you know ... it's time to start*
*something new and trust the magic of beginnings."*

– Anonymous

So you've done the research, you've learned all about the schools. Wouldn't it be nice if the colleges did as much research to get to know you? Well, unfortunately and fortunately, this is not the case. While this means that your work is far from over, it also means that you get to decide what they know about you. Remember, you have more control than you think you do.

The first thing you need to know is that admissions committees are always looking for ways to make their job easier. This is why your transcript is so important — because numbers are an easy way to compare applicants. Because of this, the college admissions process always goes back to your hard work.

# What Do Colleges Look For In Your Transcript?

- Do you have good grades?

- Do your grades improve throughout high school?

- Do you take the hardest classes available?

- Are you getting all A's in easy classes?
  Or B's in tough classes?

By the time you have the application in front of you, there is nothing you can do about the grades that are already on your transcript (which is why it is important to recognize that the college admissions process begins in the ninth grade). But you should also continue to work on your grades. NEVER let your grades slip, and even better than maintaining your grades, improve them. Colleges are happy to look at information you send them, even after you have sent in your application. Their decision is not final until you receive a letter from them.

So, what now? Now you get to use your voice. It is your job to show the admissions committee who you are, and the application is one of the ways you get to do that. Remember that, unless your mom, dad, or close relative is the dean of admissions, the admissions committee doesn't know you. They know your name and your Social Security number (which you will have memorized by the time you've filled out all your applications!), and they can't admit you based on that information alone. So, tell them! They want to know.

## Use Your Voice

- Be yourself.

- Don't exaggerate or lie.

- Be honest, genuine, and thoughtful. "Honesty comes through in an application," says Ed Hu, former admissions officer at Brown. "So does shallowness."

- Don't tell them what you think they want to hear. Tell them who you are.

 Context is very important to admissions officers — they are looking at you within the context of where you're coming from.

## What Is Your Context?

- Where are you from? A major city, a rural small town?

- What kind of high school do you attend? A prestigious private school? A parochial school? A public school?

This is the most obvious context that the admissions committee will see you in. From the very start, they look at your application next to the knowledge of this context. We call this the "group context." This information makes you part of a group, maybe New York City private schools, or rural small town public schools. You will need to stand out from the group.

# How Can You Stand Out?

- Colleges want highly motivated students, so do something you're passionate about. It could be anything from sailing to writing letters to soldiers.

- What are common activities among applicants in your group? Do something different or take your activity to the next level. Don't just play lacrosse; volunteer at an after-school lacrosse practice for underprivileged kids. Better yet, start one.

While you can't change your group, you can give the admissions officers an even better sense of your context. The more information you give them, the more that your context will define you as an individual, rather than as part of a group. If you leave the space for extracurricular activities blank with no explanation, the admissions committee will never know that the reason you have no time for soccer or painting is because you spend all your free time working to help out your family. The admissions committee wants to get to know you! They don't want to hear excuses, but they do want to hear the truth. So how do you get yourself across to the admissions committee? Here are some guidelines for filling out your application:

# Convey Who You Are

- You are not writing an instruction manual. Put your personality into your short answers. Use your real, genuine voice, not stuffy or stilted language.

- Never leave anything blank. If you don't have any awards or honors because your school doesn't give them, then say so!

- Never say that you're undecided or that you don't know. What do you think? What will best reflect who you are?

- Be specific. If you list something the admissions committee won't understand (something unique to your high school, for instance), explain it, or they'll never know.

- Highlight your strengths and minimize your weaknesses. The admissions committee knows you're not perfect, but you don't want to emphasize the areas where you are not as strong.

Another way to stand out as an individual is to maintain focus throughout your application. Focus will help admissions officers remember who you are. This is one of the reasons it is better to have a few things you are committed to, rather than 12 things you do once a month.

# Maintain Focus

- Commit time and energy to two or three activities that you really care about.

- Group related activities together under a single heading.

- Use two or three themes throughout your application to give a sense of order to otherwise miscellaneous information.

# Words of Wisdom

Jonathan Reider, former Senior Associate Director of Admissions for Stanford, tells this story: "One applicant complained to me that there were only 10 spaces on the application for extracurricular, and she had 17. I told her to just put in 10, but she insisted that they were all important to her. So, I told her to put three." It is easier to believe that three things are 'really important' to you, than 17 things. If you have 17 activities outside of school, how can you possibly have the time to truly commit to any of them?

You want to show that you are more than a list of activities or a set of grades. You want to show that you are a person with experiences, and that you can think intelligently about those experiences. Make sure to provide thoughtful answers. Know why you're telling the admissions committee something. Colleges like to see that you're insightful. Use your short answers to tell the admissions committee more about yourself than your lists can. Don't agonize over them, but give them some thought before scribbling away.

There are some other things to know about that can increase your chances of admission. No part of this process is ever a sure thing, but every little bit helps.

# APPLICATION WORDS OF WISDOM

- Your summers count. You should be prepared to do more than lounge around the beach all summer. Study abroad, get a job, do something worthwhile that will show colleges how motivated you are.

- If you have found the college of your dreams, somewhere that you are absolutely certain you want to attend, and if you have a strong transcript, you might want to apply Early Decision. By doing so, you are making a promise to attend if accepted. Remember, colleges want students who want them, so this can greatly improve your chances of admission.

- Is the college trying to develop any of its departments? Do you happen to have an interest in that department? Contact the head of the department and express your interest—the more relationships you build in this process, the better.

- Finally, the presentation of your application counts. Again, consistency is important. How can you make sure your application is in tip-top shape?

# Early Decision vs. Early Action

- **Early Decision (ED)** is binding. This means that if you are accepted, you must attend that college, and you must withdraw any applications sent to other schools. Because of this, it is best to apply ED only if you are sure about wanting to attend.

- **Early Action (EA)** is non-binding. You are not required to attend if they accept you.

- If you are a qualified student, ED will increase your chances of admission.

- For both EA and ED, you will know as early as mid-December whether you have been accepted or not. It can be a relief to be accepted early, but you must remember to keep your grades up.

# Details Count

- Finish all of your sentences. Jennifer Fondler, Dean of Admissions at Barnard College, has seen applications where it seems the applicant took a break in the middle of a question, and forgot to go back!

- Ask your English teacher to proofread your application before you send it out.

- Make several copies, for your own information, or in case your application gets lost.

# Extra Information

What if there are things you think the admissions committee should know, but that don't fit anywhere on the application? If that is the case, you have a few options:

- You can write about it in your personal essay.

- You can ask your guidance counselor to explain it in his/her letter of recommendation.

# Reading List

- **The Truth About Getting In** by Katherine Cohen, Ph.D. Cohen is definitely a businesswoman — she charges up to $29,000 for her college advising services. You can get her sensible advice for under $20 in this book.

- **How to Get Into the Top Colleges** by Richard Montauk and Krista Klein. This is an enormous reference book, easy to understand, and everything you ever wanted to know about applying to college.

# Workbook Time!

Reflect on the question posed in this chapter.
What is your context?

How can you stand out? Are there any concrete steps
you can take right now to start standing out more?

_____

_____

_____

_____

_____

_____

_____

_____

_____

_____

# Chapter 6.
# Storytime: Your Personal Essay

> *" One day I will find the right words, and they will be simple."*
>
> – Jack Kerouac

Jack is right. Your essay is a message about who you are, what you care about, how you think, and what you want. It's not about large words; it's about telling a story. A story that lets the person who might never meet you in person know who you are.

Start with telling whatever story you have chosen. Then go back and re-work it. Edit it. Read it out loud. Show it to a few (as in less than three) people for their input. Not to rewrite it, but to say if they think it represents you accurately. Is there anything they can add?

# First things first

## What Are Colleges Looking For?

- Colleges want to hear your real voice.

- Admissions officers have read hundreds of essays — they can tell the difference between a student's voice and an adult's. Your essay has to sound like a high school senior wrote it, and "the only adult I know who can sound like a 17-year-old is J.D. Salinger," says Jon Reider, former Senior Associate Director of Admissions for Stanford.

- They want to hear thoughtfulness and insight.

- They want to get a sense of who you would be as a part of their student body. Are you a fit?

- After they read your essay, they should say to themselves, "I want to meet this kid."

Okay, so it seems like you have free reign over the essay. As long as you're genuine and insightful and clear, right? Well, almost. There are a few things that you should definitely avoid when writing your essay.

# What Not To Do

- Don't preach, and don't be argumentative.

- Don't use humor if you have to try too hard, or if you're not funny.

- This might seem obvious, but don't plagiarize. You will get caught.

- Don't write about what you think admissions officers want to hear, or you will lose your oh-so-important personal voice. What they really want to hear is what you want to write about.

- Don't write about an original topic, because it's all been done. What hasn't been done is your genuine voice.

- Don't be too subtle. Admissions officers don't have the time to stop and figure it out.

- The general consensus among admissions officers and college counselors is to avoid writing about sexual experiences.

- Do not use gimmicks. They come across as silly, or worse, annoying.

- Finally, avoid the 3 OB's: Don't be Obnoxious, Obscene, or Obscure.

Well, there goes free reign. So, what can you do? Lots.

# Notes

# Chapter 7.
# Getting Started

*"The secret of getting ahead is getting started."*
**— Mark Twain**

- Look through a book of successful college essays, not to get ideas, but more to realize how many possibilities there are. This makes writing the essay a little less scary.

- Look through that journal you've been keeping for ideas.

- Do some writing exercises. Check out some helpful writing books, such as *Bird by Bird* by Anne Lamott or *Deep Writing* by Eric Maisel.

- Look through your application. What else should the admissions committee know about you that isn't conveyed there?

- Remember that you can write about almost anything. Ed Hu, former admissions officer for Brown says that he distinctly remembers an essay from 16 years ago, that was about trying to find a parking spot. "It was very simple, but by sharing his thought process, [the applicant] really told a lot about himself."

- Once you have an idea, sit down and write. Do not get stuck on a catchy title or first line—that will come later. Do not worry about spelling or grammar. Just write. This is Draft 1.

Now, remember who your audience is. Don't be intimidated by them but assume that they have been reading essays and applications for hours, with no end in sight. Assume that they know nothing about you, and they are dying to get to know you. Based on these assumptions, you can further assume that you should try to tell a story, but with that story, you must paint a clear picture of yourself. Remember that, above all, your essay needs to be about you. Admissions officers have no time to read about your pet turtle, your grandmother, or your trip to Bali. So, make sure that, if you write about how someone or something has affected you, a minimal part of your essay should be about the person or thing. The majority needs to be devoted to your reaction. The essay should always go back to you. Who are you?

## What To Do

- Tell a story, but...

- Make it about you.

- Use your genuine voice.

- Demonstrate an upbeat and positive outlook.

- Keep it simple and coherent.

- Be specific, not vague.

- Write in the first person.

Once you have your draft, you will want to step aside for a few days, even a week, before you try to revise. Don't worry too much about grammar or punctuation yet. Just focus on simplifying and clarifying your first draft. What will the admissions committee see about you in this essay? Is that what you meant to convey? You will probably have to play with and reshape your essay several times before it's just right, but hopefully by the end of the process, you will have a piece of writing that you can feel proud of.

Try to steer away from writing your essay about divorce, family death, and other things that are faced by many people. These have been overdone.

# Reading List

- **On Writing the College Application Essay** by Harry Bauld. This is a great book. It is fun to read, and it will not only help you with your college essay, but it will also improve your writing skills.

- **100 Successful Harvard Application Essays** compiled by the Harvard Independent. The best way to break down the stress over picking a topic is to see how many different kinds of essays have been successful. This is one of many compilations of college essays.

- **Bird by Bird** by Anne Lamott is fun to read, and has some great writing tips.

- **Deep Writing** by Eric Maisel. Get those creative juices flowing with this book of writing exercises.

# Workbook Time!

What excites you? What makes you who you are?

_____

_____

_____

_____

_____

_____

_____

_____

_____

_____

_____

_____

_____

Write down any formative experiences that you can write your personal statement on. What is specific to you?

_____

_____

_____

_____

_____

_____

_____

_____

_____

_____

_____

_____

# Chapter 8.
## Getting to Know You: Interviews and Letters of Recommendation

*" You will never get a second chance to make a first impression."*

— Will Rogers

## Interviews

Your essay is one way that you can really tell the admissions committee about you. Another way to do this is through an interview. Some interviews are with admissions officers, some are with alumni, and some are with currently enrolled students. And while most colleges insist that the interview won't make or break your case (unless something goes horribly wrong) they do matter on some level.

What level is that? Well, for starters, it is a good idea to think of the interview as less of an interrogation and more of a conversation. The interview is a great way for you to demonstrate your interest in the college. In fact, if the college recommends that you interview, you should at the very least try to set one up. Otherwise, you will look uninterested. Remember, colleges want students who want them. So how do you get the interview to help you the most?

# Interview Tips

- You should call to set one up. This shows that you are interested, not just your parents.

- Call two to three months in advance, especially for an on-campus interview.

- Be familiar with the information the college has sent you about itself, and its course catalog. You want to know the school well.

- Review your application. What sorts of questions are asked? The interview questions will be similar.

- Think of some questions to ask the interviewer. If you have the chance to ask questions and you decline, you seem uninterested and uninteresting. Engage the interviewer!

- If you have been keeping up on your reading, you will have plenty to talk about. It is good to come across as knowing what's going on in the world.

- Be clean and presentable.

- Don't swear. In fact, if you tend to swear often, practice talking without swearing the week before your interview.

- Turn the interview to a topic you want to talk about. It is easiest to talk about something you know well, such as your passion for fly fishing.

- Be upbeat and positive, just like you were in your essay.

# Questions You Might Be Asked

1. Tell me about yourself

2. Why are you interested in this College?

3. Why Do You Want to Major in ___?

4. What are your academic strengths?

5. What are your academic weaknesses?
   How have you addressed them?

6. What do you plan to contribute to this school

7. What do you expect to be doing 10 years from now?

8. What would you change about your high school?

9. What is your favorite book?

10. Whom do you most admire?

11. Why do you want to go to this college?

12. What do you like to do for fun?

13. What is an obstacle you've faced and how did
    you get through it?

14. What makes you unique?

*This list came from PrepScholar Blog.*

# Questions to Ask the Interviewer

1. What makes students at this university different?

2. What is something that makes you really proud to work at this university?

3. In your opinion, what are the character traits of a student who would excel here?

4. What advice would you give an incoming freshman?

5. I read in the school newspaper that students are worried about "X" issue. Can you tell me more about this?

6. How is this school addressing (insert social cause you are passionate about)?

7. I've heard about (popular/traditional event at the college). What's it like?

8. If they went to the college ask "What made you go to this college?"

9. How did going to this school help get you to where you are today?

10. What sort of internship and career placement services does the school offer?

*This content came from College Essay Guy and Indeed.*

GOOGLE is available to those who will interview you.

Do not ask the most asked questions we provide above. Tailor your question to two things. The school in which you are having an interview and your personal interest. Below are a few examples to assist you in putting them together.

Let's say your research says that 70% of the student body focus on business. That the school's known strength is around business education. But you are interested in writing. Ask questions about the writing program; is there a teacher they know about who is wonderful, or what classes in the writing arena are the students finding popular? If you have no idea what you might be majoring in, ask about the freshman options for auditing classes in subjects of interest. And, know what subjects you might find of interest, as the interviewer may ask that follow up question.

Let's say the school is a half hour from a booming metropolis, like New York City. You could ask about extracurricular activities that might take you to the city that are college sponsored. Do they offer daily transportation to museums? But if you have zero intention of leaving your campus, leave this question behind. Remember, always be you.

If you tutored in prisons during high school, ask them about where you could continue doing that when you attend. What you participated in during high school might be continued in college. Ask them about those opportunities. But only if you are truly interested. Remember, always be you.

Tell them why you find their institution interesting.

Ask them a question or two about themselves. If it comes naturally that is. Remember, always be you.

# Alumni Interviews

Sometimes, when you are not able to go to the college for an interview, the college will set up an interview with an alumnus. These are taken very seriously by admission's people. And the person who interviews you is usually active in the college alumni program and often turns out to be a strong networking connection throughout your life.

Lesson Learned: We know someone who got an interview with an alumnus at her top school, the one she was applying to early. Believe it or not, she was out late the night before, hung over, and hadn't even planned what time would get her there fifteen minutes before the interview. She breezed in, breathless, three minutes late. It went downhill from there. The interviewer was a world traveler (something she would have known had she researched who she was meeting with) and honed in on our applicant's Model United Nations participation. Is Model UN an activity of interest for this applicant? Not so much. She knew it looked good on her application forms, and it was in Boston, and turned out to be a fun weekend where she just didn't have to participate in the activities outside of social gatherings. And, the obscure country she was representing from Africa. What was its name again? Anyway, the alumni asked her what the issues were that were most important to the country she was representing and what did the team do to bring them before the model United Nations? Let's just say that even with near perfect SAT scores, perfect academic record, and recommendations that would blow your mind, she did not get in. One morning. Ill-prepared. And, she was busted. She learned her lesson.

So, five things to do before an alumni interview

1. GOOGLE the interviewer. Check out their social media.

2. Go to where you will meet and scope it out. If it's a crowded place, get there early for a table in the back.

3. Dress as you. But respectfully.

4. Prepare questions for them. How did they make their decision? What made them look at that school? How did they make the most of what was offered?

5. See if you know anyone in common. If so, decide whether to mention it or not.

6. If you are nervous, you can say so. It's an icebreaker.

7. Thank you note. As soon as you get home—before they send in their recommendation to admission. Drop it off at their house if it's not too stalky.

Okay, yes, we know our list of five in this case turned out to be seven. We think it's worth it.

If you have the opportunity to do an interview, DO IT. You want to use every chance you have to show the college that you are interested, and to show them who you are. It is a good idea to do some practice interviews. Think about the questions the interviewer will ask. If possible, schedule the interview for your favorite college last, so you have plenty of time to practice at the other schools on your list. Remember that you are not trying to impress your peers — acting too cool is a very bad idea. Their opinion could set you apart from other applicants

# Letters of Recommendation

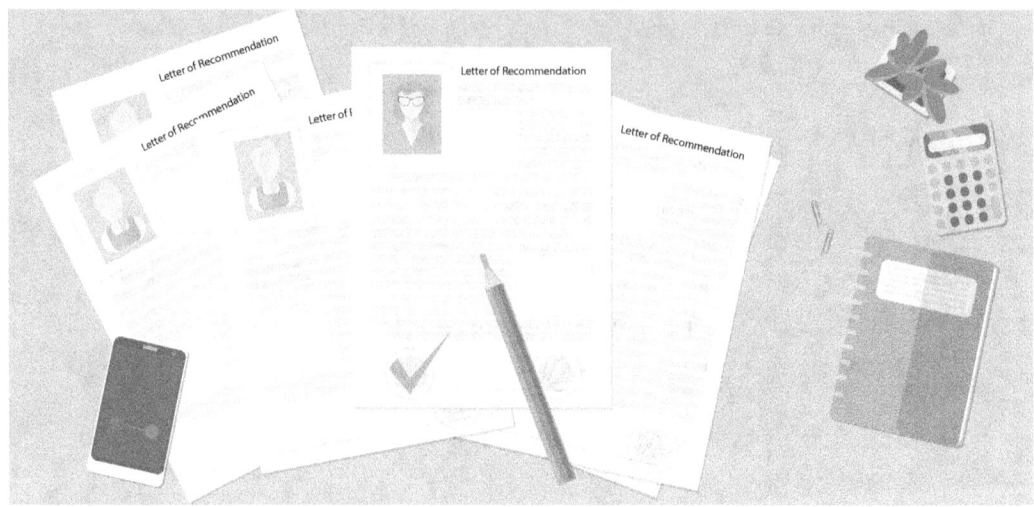

Remember our Cast of Characters? Well, here is where your teachers come in. Of course, up until now, they have played a major role in your education, second only to your own role, but now is their chance to directly influence the way the admissions committee sees you. Most colleges require 2 letters of recommendation from 2 of your teachers, and 1 from your college counselor.

How important are these letters of recommendation? Very. Your transcript is important because it shows colleges how well you have done, and whether or not you will be able to handle the course load at their school, but it doesn't say much more than that. Admissions committees also want to know: Are you enthusiastic? Motivated? Do you work well in a classroom setting? Or are you bored? Do you work just to get the grades? Do you have an attitude problem? Your teachers can give admissions committees the best insight into what kind of student you are.

So, how can you get the best letters of recommendation? Well, lucky for you, the same things that have made you a good student will help guarantee great recommendations.

# Build Relationships with Teachers

- Go to class every day.

- Participate. Ask and answer questions.

- Be enthusiastic about your classes. Your teachers will notice.

- Get to know your teachers. Go to them outside of class for help, or to discuss something from class.

- Ask for letters of recommendation from teachers who know you well, and who are good writers.

- Your most recent teachers are also the most credible.

# Advice from an Expert

- When thinking about who you want to ask. Think about someone who knows you very well, they will be able to speak about you best.

- Give them plenty of time to write your recommendation.

- It is best to ask in person. Sending an email is too informal and not personal.

- Inform them what schools you are applying to.

- Tell them who else is writing a letter of recommendation for you and what they will be highlighting in their letters. Additionally, provide a resume to remind them of what you do outside of their class. This will help them speak to your academic self and personal self.

- If it has been weeks since you asked and nothing has been submitted, follow up and include the due date.

- Once you have received their letter of recommendation, send a note that it has been received and thank them for taking the time to write the letter. They are busy people, especially during application season, a thank you goes a long way.

- Keep them updated on the process. Share admissions, deferrals, waitlistings, and rejections.

- Share with them where you end up deciding to go. They are a part of your posse and they want to see you succeed!

*" Don't just ask "will you write a rec for me." Ask me if I think I can speak highly of you and your work. And help me remember some highlights."*
**—Meg Donnelly**

*" Let me share the joy of your decision of where to go!"*
**—Meg Donnelly**

When you ask your teacher to write you a recommendation, give them the chance to decline. Don't force the issue. If they would rather not write your recommendation, there is probably a reason. Find someone who will gladly write you a stellar recommendation. If you have trouble doing this, then you haven't been doing your job to be the best student you can be.

Getting a great recommendation from your college counselor is not much different than getting one from your teachers. You will want to initiate and maintain a relationship with your counselor, starting in your freshman year. This is especially important since they will not have the chance to see you in action in your classes. Also, make sure that you ask your counselor to address any issues in their letter that are important for the admissions committee to understand your context. While you could explain these things in an addendum of your own, it is possible that such a thing could come across as making excuses. If you are worried about this possibility, it is in your best interest that your college counselor addresses them.

## 5 THINGS TO REMEMBER WHEN ASKING SOMEONE TO WRITE A LETTER OF RECOMMENDATION

1) Check the college application because many schools require letters from specific teachers.

2) Be sure to select a teacher from your junior year because it is important that admissions officers have an idea of who you are currently, not a few years ago.

3) Make sure you give your teacher/counselor/coach a lot of time to complete it, they most likely have many of these recommendations to write for other students on top of their teaching workload.

4) Feel free to ask coaches, employers and other people who can speak to your character and who know you well.

5) Be polite and kind. Don't forget to thank them, ask if they have any questions or need any other material to complete the recommendation. And finally, don't forget to follow up, thanking them for their support and for their recommendation.

*Content from BigFuture College Board.*

# Helpful Websites

- https://blog.prepscholar.com/college-interview-questions-you-should-prepare-for

- https://www.collegeessayguy.com/blog/questions-college-interview

- https://www.indeed.com/career-advice/interviewing/questions-for-college-interviewer

- https://bigfuture.collegeboard.org/plan-for-college/college-prep/stand-out/how-to-get-a-great-letter-of-recommendation

- Waive your right to view your letter of recommendation.This implies to admissions that these letters are more legitimate and trustworthy.

- In addition to teachers, think of other adults in your life like coaches, mentors, family friends that know you well that could speak to your brilliant character.

- Pick someone who could tell a real story about you. Colleges are looking for stories and personal experiences about you.

# Workbook Time!

Right now, can you think of anyone you want to ask to write you a letter of recommendation? Write their names below.

_____

_____

_____

_____

_____

Write down some ways you can strengthen your relationships with teachers.

_____

_____

_____

_____

_____

_____

_____

Given all of the information we just gave you, what are some questions you want to ask in your interview?

_____

_____

_____

_____

_____

_____

_____

_____

_____

# Chapter 9.
# It Ain't Over 'Til It's Over:
# What's Next

*" Patience is not simply the ability to wait – it's how we behave while we're waiting."*

— Joyce Meyer

Your applications are sent out. Now all you can do is sit and wait, right? Wrong. Make sure that you maintain or improve your grades throughout your senior year. Continue to participate in your extracurricular activities. Colleges will receive your final transcript, and if they don't like what they see, there is the possibility they will retract an offer of admission. Don't risk it.

So what do you do when you have the college's letter in hand?

Well, this all depends on what they have to say. If you have been accepted—Congratulations!—and you choose to attend, you will want to respond, as well as send in your Deposit. You will want to notify the other schools that you are declining their offer of admission.

What if you don't receive the much-anticipated letter of acceptance? Don't despair. You still have options. If you are waitlisted, you will want to send a letter to the office of admissions, letting them know of your continued interest in their school. You will also want to maintain contact with them, sending any new relevant information. However, do not assume that you will be accepted off the waitlist. You should put a deposit in at another school, ensuring that, come September, you will have a school to attend.

Hopefully by this point you will have a few colleges that have accepted you. Your job now is to choose where you want to go. This may be an easy decision for some if there is 1 school that stood out. However, if you are weighing the pros and cons of different schools, go back to your notes in previous sections. What were you looking for in a college? Look over your notes that you took during your tours of those schools. What stood out? Where do you see yourself? Can you picture yourself being happy and successful there?

# From One Parent to Another About the Admission's Process

I remember hearing some friends refer to "we are applying to colleges now...." At first, although this thought quickly subsided, I thought they were returning to school along with their senior children. And, then it hit. Some parents are too invested in this search for a college. Way too invested. Things to remember...

- This is their journey, and you are a cheerleader along the way. An advisor if asked. A sounding board. A tour guide on the college visits. You are the adjective, not the noun. You are in the background, not in the front of the line. On a college tour, you are behind your child, not asking questions from the first row.

- This is their first foray into decisions—life changing decisions—that they must make on their own.

- Trust them. Tell them you know they will get it right, and that they should trust their gut.

- If you have done your job of raising a strong, sure-footed human, then it will be fine. If you have not, then it's the first lesson they will learn on the way to emancipation from their bondage to your vision for their future.

- It's hard to keep your mouth shut. Oh so hard. It's also the most loving thing you can do. Good luck. And believe in yourself that you can step back, perhaps for the first time, and say to your fabulous child, "You've got this. Tell me how I can help."

# Workbook Time!

How can you maintain your grades? Make a list below of the classes you have and how you can maintain or improve your grades. This could be going to office hours for support or making a study group with your friends. Whatever you think will help, jot it down below.

_____

_____

_____

_____

_____

_____

_____

_____

_____

_____

# Chapter 10.
# You're In, What's Next??

*" None is more impoverished than the one who has no gratitude. Gratitude is a currency that we can mint for ourselves and spend without fear of bankruptcy."*
— **Fred De Witt Van Amburgh**

By now you have been accepted and committed to a college. YAY!!! Your hard work paid off. But remember, this wasn't possible without your posse and your support system. Be sure to thank every single person who helped you along this journey. We don't mean shoot them a text saying "thanks," we mean write out a full letter thanking them for the specific things they have done to get you where you are now. This will be unique for each person. These letters will be most personal if they are handwritten.

## Next Steps

Take a look at your course catalog for your freshman year. The sooner you do this the better because when it comes time to pick classes you will know exactly what you want to take. This is the last thing you need to do, we promise.

Finally, Enjoy! You have just crossed the finish line of the college admissions process and you have come out on top! You deserve to celebrate and enjoy the remaining part of your senior year of high school but try not to rob a bank or get caught for drunk and disorderly conduct.

## Workbook Time!

Take this space to reflect! You have just completed the college admissions process. How do you feel? What have you learned about yourself through this process?

_____

_____

_____

_____

_____

_____

_____

# Chapter 11.
## The Money Tree: How to Pay for College

*" Impossible only means that you haven't found the solution yet."*

                                                        **–Anonymous**

Did you know that most students are on some sort of financial aid? College is expensive, and most families will need to seek outside help in making such a major investment. What do you need to do to obtain financial aid? There are some basic steps you will need to take.

# Paperwork

- Your very first step is to contact the college's financial aid offices to find out which forms they require. Just the basic forms? Do they have supplementary forms?

- Fill out the FAFSA form. You can find it at www.fafsa.ed.gov. This form determines how much money your family will be expected to contribute. The FAFSA is released on October 1st, and you should fill it out the year before you plan to attend college. But the sooner you fill it out the better. Different schools may have different deadlines so be sure to check with your specific school.

- Once you have determined your list of colleges, register for a Profile at cssprofile.collegeboard.org.

- As with everything, make several copies of the forms before you send them.

How can you get the best financial aid package possible? Well, this depends on your unique situation. A private financial aid advisor says that the truth is, you will have the hardest time receiving a generous financial aid package if you are from a middle or upper-middle class family. If this is you, you will need to shape the way your family looks on paper to your best advantage. The process of filling out financial aid forms is not very different from filing out taxes: for any question, there are several right answers. The trick is to use the answer that will help you most, and is at the same time auditable and true. IF you need financial aid, and you can afford a financial aid advisor, you should probably hire one–they will be able to help you best shape your financial profile to get you the best financial aid package possible.

# Other Ways to Improve Your Aid Package

- Research. Find out the average amount of debt for graduated students. If their average debt is lower, you are more likely to receive a better financial aid package from that school. Different schools have different aid.

- Go to your school's website. They will have a tab or link to scholarship and grant options

- Negotiate. Don't be afraid to show a college your better financial aid package from another college. They may or may not meet the better package, but you have nothing to lose — they won't take away what they've already given you.

- If a college truly has not met your needs, go to the financial aid office and explain your situation. Even if they won't give you more grants (free money), they will probably give you more loans.

# Grants and Scholarships

In addition to financial aid, many schools offer grants and scholarships. These forms of aid are different for every school so be sure to research what your specific school offers. The University of Michigan offers Four Year Renewable Scholarships, but you must apply before the academic year. While scholarship and grant deadlines differ by school, don't wait until you are attending the university to figure this out. Start right when you have been admitted so you don't miss these crucial deadlines.

# Reading List

- ***College Financial Aid for Dummies*** by Herm Davis. This is an easy-to-read book of all the basics.

- ***Meeting College Costs*** by Deb Thyng Schmidt. This is a sort of handbook for your family to figure out how to pay for college.

- ***Don't Miss Out*** by Anna Leider. This book is a fun read (considering the topic), and delves into how to make financial aid work for you.

# Helpful Websites

- FAFSA: www.fafsa.ed.gov

- Fill out the PROFILE at cssprofile.collegeboard.org

- Everything you ever wanted to know about financial aid: www.finaid.org

- Search for scholarships at www.fastaid.com

# Chapter 12.
# Breaking News: Affirmative Action, AI and More

## Equality

*" Not everyone is showing up with the same equipment."*

–Christine Merser

# Affirmative Action

In June 2023 the Supreme Court overturned affirmative action in college admissions. This means that it will be illegal to consider race in the evaluation of an individual's college application. This will drastically impact the admissions process, undermining the substantial disadvantage that people of color face due to systemic racism in the United States. Now, people of color will have to fight even harder to get into college.

This ruling has sparked a conversation about whether legacy admissions should also be banned. In most cases, legacy admissions decrease diversity because legacy applicants come from primarily white, upper class families.

With all of this coming into light it is hard to know how to navigate it as a college applicant. We can't give you the most updated information because it is constantly changing but here are five questions to ask Google before turning your application in, so you aren't in a position to be discounted.

1.  How do I handle affirmative action in my college application?

2.  Should I write about my race and identity in my personal statement for college applications?

3.  Should I include clubs and extracurricular activities that I was a part of that indicate my race or identity in my college application?

4.  How is [insert school name] handling affirmative action today in their college admissions?

5.  How is (insert name of school) handling legacy admissions in their college admissions today?

It's scary not knowing how this will impact the future of college admissions, but it is important that you know what is going on in the college admissions world right now. Being knowledgeable about what is going on in the admissions process and asking these 5 questions before submitting will make you the most informed college applicant you can be.

# AI in College Admissions

Really, at this point, not to be confused with months from now when it might all change, the use of AI will be used more by the colleges than you. They will use it to filter through applications and make the process of reviewing applications easier. You, as the applicant, should not be using it as much. Although, as we discussed in Chapter 4, you can use AI to help you build your college list.

## Five things to be aware of when using AI in college applications

1. Do not copy and paste responses from AI into your college application. AI spits out the same response to questions posed in similar ways. You do not want to submit an application with an identical essay to another or many other applicants.

2. AI can assist you in building your college list. Many resources like College Raptor use Artificial Intelligence to examine a student's academic record, extracurricular activities, interests and financial background and make recommendations that align with that student's situation.

3. Use AI resources to check your application for grammatical and structural errors.

4. AI can help as you get ready to go on college campus tours. What if you don't know what questions you want to ask during your tour? There is a feature on ChatGPT called "Act as." You can ask AI to act as a potential student of, for example, the University of North Carolina. So what you would do is type in "Act as a potential student of the University of North Carolina who is visiting campus. I am interested in (insert your areas of interest). What are some potential questions to ask the tour guide during my visit?" This will give you more personalized questions that will give you more insight on how you would fit in at that specific college.

5. While AI is incredibly useful and can help in your research and writing, it is not perfect. AI is trained on data and that data has the potential to be biased. Remember that if you choose to use it during your application process.

**Remember that college admissions faculty can use AI too to help them cut down the application pool.**

# Helpful Websites

- www.sageridge.org/about/news/details/~board/news/post/ai-in-college-admissions-how-chatgpt-and-other-generative-ai-programs-reshaping-higher-education-admission-decisions-practices

- www.forbes.com/sites/avivalegatt/2023/04/24/how-to-boost-your-college-applications-using-ai---without-cheating-the-essay

- https://podcasts.apple.com/ca/podcast/affirmative-action-for-the-1-percent/id1200361736?i=1000622502681

# Notes

_____

_____

_____

_____

_____

_____

_____

_____

# Chapter 13.
# Year-by-Year Timeline

*"Little by little, one travels far."*

—J.R.R. Tolkien

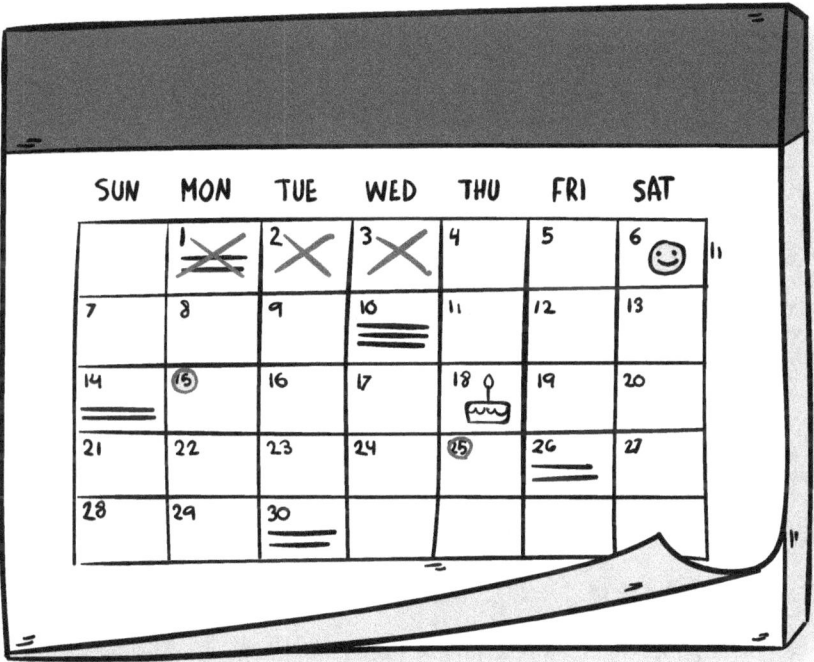

# Every Year

- Read, read, read!

- Keep up with the extracurricular activities you started in 9th grade or before.

- Take the most challenging courses you can, while maintaining good grades.

- Keep a journal (it will come in handy later for essay ideas).

# Freshman Year

- Develop a few extracurricular activities that you enjoy. Karate? Tapestry weaving?

# Sophomore Year

- Take any relevant AP tests. (May)

# Junior Year

- Start to research colleges (see Chapter 2).

- Take the PSAT. (October)

- Register to take the March SAT or ACT. (January)

- Set up interviews for your Spring Break visits to Colleges. (February)

- Take the SAT or ACT (see Chapter 3). (March)

- Register for any relevant June SAT or ACT tests.

- Visit colleges during your Spring Break (see Chapter 4)

- Set up interviews for your summer visits to colleges. (April)

- Take relevant AP tests. Take the SAT or ACT again if necessary (register upon receiving scores from March tests. (May)

- Visit colleges. (Summer)

- Start working on your personal essay.

- Request applications from colleges.

- Register for the October SAT or ACT if necessary.

# Senior Year

- Take the SAT or ACT again if necessary. (October)

- Deadline for most EA and ED applications. (November)

- Deadline for most Regular Decision applications. (December)

- File FAFSA form (see Chapter 10).

- Receive letters of acceptance! (April)

# Chapter 14.
# The Finish Line: What Comes Next?

*" Success is not the destination, but the journey."*
— Arthur Ashe

You made it! If you've worked through this book, you've taken a huge step toward navigating the complex world of college admissions with confidence, clarity, and purpose. The application process can be daunting, but it's also an opportunity to reflect on who you are, what you want, and how you can shape your future.

## Looking Back: What You've Accomplished

Think about everything you've done in this process— researching schools, writing essays, preparing for tests, seeking recommendations, and putting together the best possible application. More than that, you've learned valuable life skills: time management, self-reflection, and the ability to advocate for yourself. These are tools that will serve you well far beyond the college admissions process.

## What's Next?

No matter where you are in your admissions journey—waiting for decisions, weighing offers, or planning your next steps— remember that your college choice is not the end-all, be-all of your success. What truly matters is what you do with the opportunities ahead of you. College is just one part of a bigger picture, and your growth, relationships, and experiences will define your future more than the name on your diploma.

# A Few Final Pieces of Advice

Stay Open-Minded. You may not get into your first-choice school, but every college has unique opportunities. Keep an open mind. We often hear stories of students who didn't attend their first-choice school, and it ended up being the best decision of their lives—whether because of the people they met or the opportunities they received.

Keep Perspective. College admissions can feel like the biggest challenge of your life, but in reality, it's just one of many steps toward your future.

Embrace the Journey. Wherever you land, your success will be shaped by your passion, curiosity, and willingness to make the most of your experiences.

## Pay It Forward

If you've found this book helpful, consider passing it on. Help a younger sibling, a friend, or a classmate who is just starting this process. Share what you've learned. Support one another. The college admissions process is competitive, but it doesn't have to be isolating. Lift others up as you climb.

## The Best is Yet to Come

The road to college is full of twists, turns, and unexpected moments—but trust that you're exactly where you're supposed to be. You've put in the effort, and now it's time to step forward into the next chapter of your life with confidence.

We would love to hear where you end up. Send us an email at Inquiry@ApricityPublishing.com if you'd like to share anything about your college journey that you think could help those who go through it next.

Congratulations, and good luck!

—The College Admissions Handbook Team